"My Body is Safe" by Crystal Hardstaff
Published by The Gentle Counsellor

2023

Queensland, Australia

www.thegentlecounsellor.com

hello@thegentlecounsellor.com

Second Edition 2024

For any inquiries please contact Crystal Hardstaff at @thegentlecounsellor or hello@thegentlecounsellor.com

My body is safe, that's what I know
I get to decide who can touch me, so
I'll listen to my heart, tummy, and brain
And if I feel scared, I'll say it again.

Notes for Parents, Caregivers, and People who work with Children

It is important to teach children about tricky people and safe people as part of their personal safety education. In the past, the term "stranger danger" was commonly used, but this approach has since been updated to focus on identifying and avoiding tricky people, who may not always be strangers.

Here are some tips on how to teach children about tricky people and safe people:

1. **Start the conversation early:** It is never too early to start teaching your child about personal safety. Use age-appropriate language and teach your child to trust their instincts.
2. **Use everyday examples:** Look for opportunities in everyday situations to teach your child about tricky people and safe people.
3. **Teach them about boundaries:** Teach your child that they have the right to say "no" to any touch that makes them uncomfortable. Help them understand that their body belongs to them, and no one has the right to touch them inappropriately.
4. **Practice scenarios:** Role-play different scenarios with your child, such as what to do if a stranger approaches them or what to do if someone tries to touch them inappropriately.
5. **Emphasise the importance of telling a trusted adult:** Teach your child that if someone makes them feel uncomfortable or if they encounter a tricky person, they should tell a trusted adult immediately.

By teaching your child about tricky people and safe people, you are empowering them with the knowledge and skills to stay safe. Remember to have open and ongoing conversations with your child about personal safety, and to always prioritise their well-being.

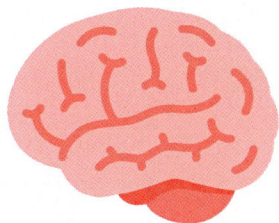

My body is special, it belongs to me,
I choose who can touch it, and that's the key.

Tricky people can look like anyone we meet,
They might offer treats, toys, or a sweet,
But if they make us feel scared or unsure,
We can trust our instincts and feel more secure.

Some people are tricky, they may seem nice,
But I trust my heart, tummy, and brain's advice.

Safe people are those who make us feel good,
They listen, respect, and help as they should,
We can go to them when we need help or care,
They'll always keep me safe, I know they'll be there.

If we ever feel scared or not sure what to do
A safe person will listen to me and you.

My heart may beat fast when I meet someone new,
Or my tummy might feel queasy, warning me too,
My brain might tell me to stop and think,
And it's okay to listen and trust that instinct.

My body is mine, and I keep it safe,
With my heart, tummy, and brain as my guide,
I have the power to stay safe.

I'll keep my private parts covered and out of sight
And I'll say "no" if something doesn't seem right.
It's important to speak up and have a voice
Because my body is mine, and that's my choice.

We'll learn to say "stop" and walk away,
And tell a safe person what happened that day.

Remember, it's always okay to say "no",
And to trust our instincts that help us as we grow.
Stay safe and happy, and enjoy life too,
We're in charge of our body, mind, and all we do.

My safe person listens to me and helps me feel okay
Because they love me, and want me safe every day.

One activity that can help children identify their instincts is called the "Feeling Check-In".

Ask the child to close their eyes and take a few deep breaths. Then, ask them to focus on how their body feels. Ask them to name any feelings or sensations they notice in their body, such as a fluttery feeling in their tummy or a tightness in their chest.

Next, explain that these feelings are their instincts, and they are there to help keep them safe. Encourage the child to pay attention to these feelings and trust them when they encounter situations that make them feel uncomfortable or unsafe.

You can also ask the child to draw or write about their feelings to help them better understand and communicate their instincts. This activity can be done regularly to help the child become more aware of their body's signals and how to trust and act on them.

My Instincts

WHAT DOES MY BODY TELL ME?

OTHER BOOKS BY
CRYSTAL HARDSTAFF

The 'My Body' Series includes *'My Body is Mine'*, *'My Body, My Choice'*, and *'My Body is Safe'* by Crystal Hardstaff. These books are written for toddlers and young children to be introduced to and help them understand important topics such as the names of their private parts, body safety, consent, tricky people and safe people, and listening to their instincts. This book series was adapted and shortened from the author's original book *'Tricky People'* which covers all these topics and is suitable for young children to school-age.

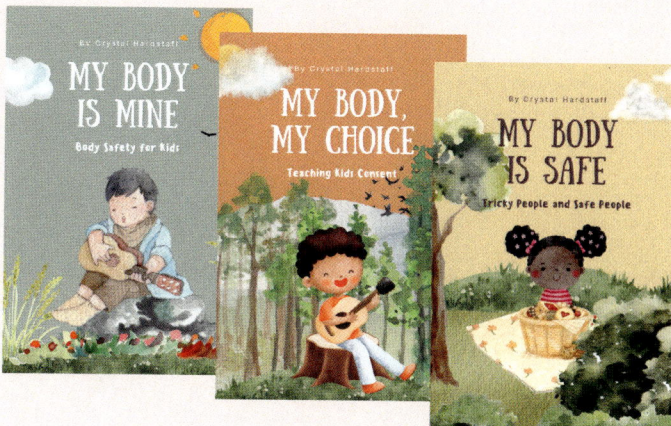

For more information visit
www.thegentlecounsellor.com

Made in the USA
Middletown, DE
25 July 2025

11227677R00018